SHADOW
&
SHINE

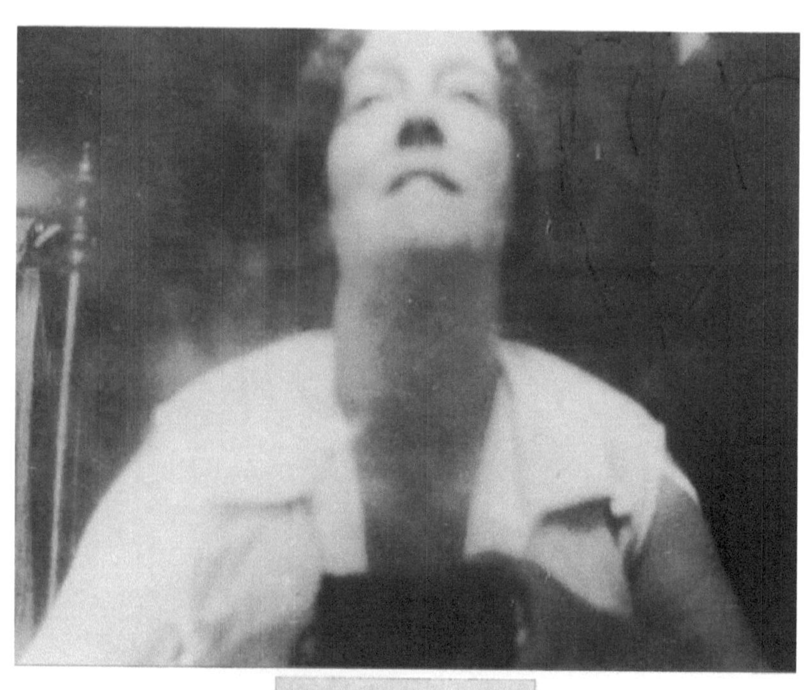

Snap shot taken
by self in mirror

a pet dove
was on my
left shoulder
but it jumped
off just as the
snap was taken

SHADOW AND SHINE:

POEMS

By

Ethel Archer.

Author of “The Whirlpool”, “Phantasy and Other Poems”, Etc.

Fainting Couch Books
2014

"Shadow and Shine is Life"
-Motto from an old sundial.

(2023 Paperback edition)
ISBN: 978-1-365-39805-6

CONTENTS

*These poems are currently non-extant.

INTRODUCTION

"Thanks so much for your poem. It is more your old self again. In it you have largeness - the same passion that swells the breast of the sea, the jealous love that sends lowering clouds, and the scorching passion of a desert sun. I think this is conveyed by the modesty of expression. It is of the Gods you sing the best."

- Eugene Wieland to Ethel Archer
July 17th, 1915.

Found among the papers of the English poet Ethel Archer (1885-1961) was a typed table of contents for a book of poems that she intended to be titled either *Fritto Misto*, an allusion to an Italian medley of small fried pieces of meat, seafood, and vegetables; or *Shadow and Shine*, after a motto she read on an old sundial. The poems she chose can be seen as fitting either title. Broken down into five sections: Philosophical Poems, Love Poems, Pastoral Poems, Various Poems, and Religious and Mystical Poems; they represent a retrospective look at her work from the pantheistic lyrics of her youth to her later Christian-inspired verses.

I chose to use her "alternative title" of *Shadow and Shine* for this collection as, rather than simply being a delightful blend of ingredients, they present the reader with a landscape of dark and light imagery, populated by humans, divinities, and personifications of the forces of nature. In these poems one finds paeans to life in all its wonders alongside dirges of death and its final sublimity.

Ethel Archer is perhaps best known for her close association with the occultists/poets Aleister Crowley and Victor Neuburg. Rather remarkably, given Crowley's fractious nature and penchant for alienating his former associates, she managed to remain friends with both men even after they had gone their separate ways.

In the early 1910s Archer and her husband, the artist/writer Eugene Wieland, worked at the offices of Crowley's biannual journal, *The Equinox: The Review of Scientific Illuminism*, to which she contributed poems and reviews. The couple's involvement in the journal soon deepened, and for a time Wieland became its publisher, with a number of issues appearing under his eponymous imprint. Archer left a semi-fictional, but apparently very accurate, account of those heady times with Crowley and Neuburg and others at the offices of *The Equinox* in her novel *The Hieroglyph* (Denis Archer, 1932).

The couple themselves, and their great romance, was the subject of a touching narrative by the writer Elizabeth Robins Pennell, who chronicled her own observation of the two in their apartment from her window. The consequent article, entitled "Les Amoureux: An Idyl of a London Garret," was published in the June 1911 issue of *The Century Magazine.* After Wieland's death at the Battle of Loos in 1915, Pennell wrote a short but powerful remembrance, *The Lovers* (William Heinemann, 1917), which told the story of his last days through the letters he sent home to his wife.

Ethel Archer's later life saw her continued involvement in the literary world, writing poems, essays, reviews, and doing translation work for various magazines and publishers.

After reconnecting with Victor Neuburg in 1930, she published a selection of her works, *Phantasy & Other Poems,* at his Vine Press.

In regards to her bibliography, she is also often cited as the author of *The Book of Plain Cooking* (A.Treherne, 1904). This book, however, was most likely written by a different "Ethel Archer." In the author's preface she states that she has twenty years of experience "directing and occasionally doing the cookery of a modest establishment," which would have had our "Ethel Archer," born in 1885, cooking a year before her own birth! No matter how implausible, I love the idea! It would certainly have fitted comfortably with the first possible title for the present selection of poems, *Fritto Misto*.

And it would be fantastic to find a forgotten book written by Ethel Archer, overlooked in an old bookshop or a manuscript randomly cataloged in a university archive with other obscure papers. All this brings us back to the volume at hand, her own outline for a collection of poems, which has languished forgotten among her papers for several decades, waiting to be assembled.

Many of the earlier poems appeared in magazines, such as *The Occult Review, The English Review*, and *The Equinox*; or in her own small volume of verse, *The Whirlpool* (Wieland, 1911), while other later works survived in manuscript or typescript.

Of exceptional note for their provenance are the manuscript poems "Death! The Miser," "Elf Song," and "The Poet Speaks," which were found in a hand-bound booklet as submissions to the Festival of Great Britain in 1951. On the front cover she wrote:

"I afterwards learned they had entered the poems under the name of "Wieland." Of course they were not even commended, but it has been suggested that the last verse of "The Poet Speaks" damned me. If that is so I am quite unrepentant. None of these poems has been sent elsewhere."

Although not originally intended for publication in this book of poems, I have appended Ethel Archer's short essay "Recollections," as yet another example of her work that, deserving of publication in her own time, never saw print.

In common with most poets, Archer often

made multiple copies of her poems for submission to different books, competitions, and journals, and it seems highly likely that yet more of her works - both unpublished and in print - are still out there to be found.

It is my hope that she would have been pleased to see this particular collection come to light.

In her introduction to *Phantasy and Other Poems* Ethel Archer suggested that her works were best appreciated when read aloud. So as you read this book, might I suggest that you give voice again to her words, let the rhythms of her poems push back the veil of years, and enjoy this lost project from the past.

-Philip R. Jensen
2014

ACKNOWLEDGEMENTS

Many thanks to Keith Richmond for his help with the Introduction and for tracking down some of the more elusive poems. And, as always, to my wife Kelly for her kind support and patience.

-PRJ

"My obligations are due to The Equinox, from which several of these poems are reprinted."

-Ethel Archer
(The Whirlpool)

"My obligations are due to the English Review and the Occult Review from which some of these poems are reprinted."

-Ethel Archer
(undated typescript)

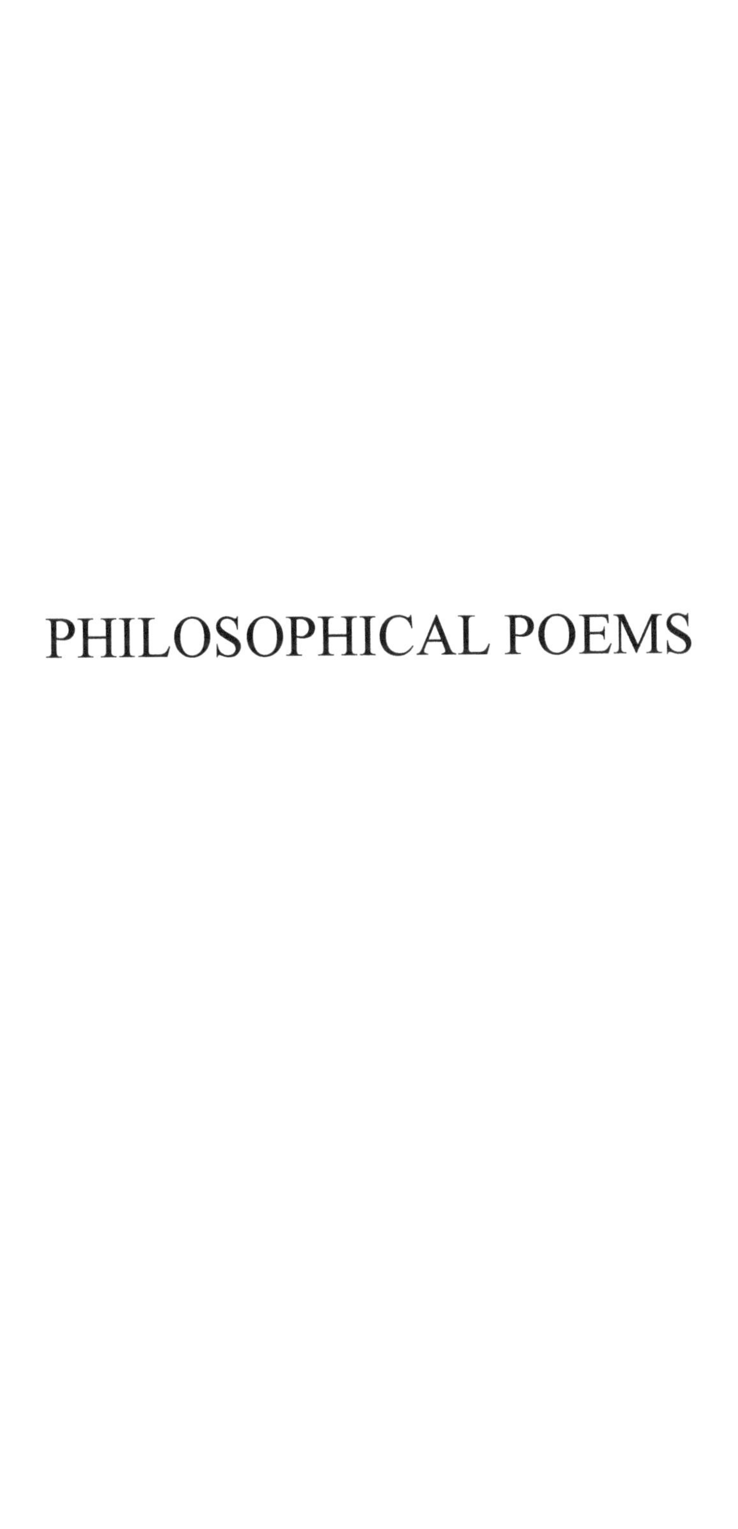

PHILOSOPHICAL POEMS

To a Skull Amongst the Roses

Within her wanton's lap where Summer showers
    Roses, red, riotous as early Spring,
    Her golden glory faint and blossoming
With more than mortal beauty, magic hours
Faint with the fragrance of a thousand flowers
    Steeped in the soul of Music –silencing
    All other sound than that which Sleep may bring
To breathing Beauty; - there the Death's-Head glowers!
    Yea! Death grins charnel-wise! His jaws half ope,
    Laugh at that lure, the shining silken rope
Vanity fashions. O'er the sockets deep
Her web she weaveth, that no man may peep
    Further in quest of Knowledge than the scope
Of Life's dimensions, so – the end is – Sleep.

Yea! Sleep for all! And how shall one foretell
The Dream's awakening! Answer! It is well
    All ye who slumber silent in the dark
    Dead halls of Hela! Do ye wake to mark
Despair's long journey through the deaf'ning swell
    Of lost Endeavour? Formless shapes embark
    Strange foes to capture? Or, remain ye stark
To dust returning? Say! O Sentinel!
    Ye answer not! Nor would ye an ye could
    Great uninvited One, whose jaws have stood
For all time open, and whose orbs are filled
With strange blind knowledge, that has ever stilled
    Those who have sought it, and have seeking viewed
What lies beyond, too late! For so ye willed.

Yea! Smile on ever! Hold thy secret yet,
    Seeing full well that no man shall return
    To wrest it from thee! Let the roses burn
In sweet confusion, and the winds forget
All things save passion and the faint regret
    That follows closest joy. And whilst we yearn
    For that we trow not, but would ever learn
More and yet more of – Know! We shall not fret!
    Warm glows the West, - and in that ruby fire
    Red roses burn sweet incense to the pyre
Of fallen Day. Pure flaming hearts obsessed
By perfumed passion – subtly manifest
    As songs that stir that soul-vibrating lyre,
Whose music is the deep Sea's heart at rest!

Appeared in ***The Whirlpool.***

A Ballad of Bedlam

Out from the windswept hollows of the Tomb
Into the Night, -
Impenetrable gloom
Folding me in from sound and sense and sight;
No Light,
Save from that leprous orb men call the Moon,
Whose rune
Spells Death and Madness:
Like to a blinded babe from out the womb,
Like a dishevelled ghost before the tomb,
I wandered seeking for my Self, the Doom
Of Ancient Days was on me.

Not a star
Swam in the heavens,- but aloft, afar,
One Meteor
Rolled like a great gold goblet through the sky,
Spilling strange dreams.
Strange dreams that ever flow, yet flow amiss,
The while a slow voice whispers: "This, perchance, then
        This!"
Yet never comes the *right* one.

Time is ended.
Time and Eternity with Fate have blended
Mine awful Destiny:-
"To watch for ever.
For ever watch, nor see the blind endeavour
Of battling with the soul that wills Eclipse.

"Ever to know.
And yet to know not ever
The thing that irks thee most, how to dissever
Thy Self from the blind wraith that watches thee.

"This deed undone, that is before thee ever!
There is No Time, thou canst forget it never,
The Thing Undone is as the Thing Before.
An endless chain, they stretch before thee, ever
Mocking thy soul with purblind hopes that shiver
As salt sea-spray on ice-bound rocks beneath.

"Laugh! For I bid thee laugh.
I bid thee mangle
These unborn babes of thine,
These hopes that dangle
Like fond fair lilies o'er a lost lagoon:
Witch-trees of innocence it sure would tangle
In subtler mesh than those strange weeds that strangle
Lost swimmers in the foul Sargasso Sea!"

I shut me up. I builded me a Tower
To hide me from the laughter of the world.
I said: "They shall not lure me from my bower
To where their love, a lecherous snake, is curled:
A Basilisk-snake that plays upon the sward,
Writhing in slow obedience to its lord.

"What if the Day be long, the Night be cheerless?
Is not an universe within my brain?
Is not the high will strong, the strong will fearless?
All I have built, shall I not build again?
Some other Universe where All is One.
Where One is All I am, and I Am – None!

"Words! 'Tis ever words, and I am stranded
With words, and tangled skeins of Things to Be.
Each word denies a word, and all are branded
Within my brain, and I must strive to see
The subtly sneering forms, the leering faces
Of words each word calls up. For me, No Grace is."

Appeared in ***The Equinox Vol. I No. X*** and ***The English Review*** (November 1919).

The Maelstrom

Beyond that outer space which bounds the blue,
Beyond the confines of the furthest star,
Beyond all thought and sight, where comets bar the light,
But myriad motes the sunlight filters through, -
Vaster than Time or Space, madly the planets race
From ever widening circles drawn afar
As drifting spar,
Down to the whirling centre: there anew
To be cast forth, till haply lost to view
In that one Eye, which is the vortex.

Narrow the circles to resurging fire!
Stars battle blindly in that dim abyss!
See in the whirling tide, as one vast suicide,
Creation stagger! Yet the one desire,
Ever insatiate, must darkly gravitate
To that deep centre, till it comes to this:
Failing, we miss.
Missing, by that same failure we acquire
One chance the more, - so vainly we aspire
To gain our final goal – perfection.

So far is comprehended. But one Eye
Of the All-Seeing holds our Universe.
Great though to Man the Storm, 'tis but a shadow-form
Slow-passing in that centre. How descry
Of that deep Eye, the Soul, the structure of the whole,
The meaning of the Maelstrom, or that terse
Tremendous curse

By some called Destiny? The eternal “Why?”
Mayhap is answered when Infinity
Becomes at last the Finite, and – the End.

Appeared in ***The Whirlpool.***

The Vampire

I dream in strange laughterless mazes;
I wake at the set of the sun;
All poppied the paean of praise is
That lives on the lives it has won.
And crimson grow cheeks that are ashen,
And gold gleam the locks that are grey,
For I live – and bright blood is my passion,
Hot-veined in the heart of the day!

Aha! For the rapture that dazes!
Wine-drained as the breast of a nun
Droops the throat that my savage soul raises,
Thirsting yet for the life that is done!
Sharp as rocks where strong billows have thundered,
Calm as seas where strange tempests have run,
Strong as Death; where the Derelicts sundered
Feed the Soul without Hope, which is One.

In the Vault of the Infinite Spaces,
By the Moon of a mirrorless Sea,
I lie, while Eternity races –
Dream-bound in the visions of me.
See poppied lips pale in the star-light,
The lustiest swoon at my breath,
Till the were-wolves howl – ho 'tis the far light!
Even so – I caress – it is Death!

Appeared in ***The Equinox Vol. I No. V.***

The Wisdom of Folly

Folly, child of the fairies born in June,
Her sweet bells jingling to a joyous tune,
Sought the dark depths of Knowledge. By the pool
She lay disrobed, and in the waters cool
Saw *still* her own reflection. Wearied soon,
Deeper she sought to fathom and to school
Her idle thoughts to Wisdom; so to rule
The world by Folly, - from sad cares immune!

A peacock's feather (late her scepter gay)
Smiling she fashions as a rod to play
At fishing. For the stagnant pool is deep,
And Folly shudders at the things which creep
Below the surface; where pale lilies sway, -
Frail, starlike blossoms, wrapt in soulless Sleep.

Appeared in ***The Whirlpool*** and as a manuscript.

The Dreamer

In the grey dim Dawn where the Souls Unborn
May look on the Things to Be;
A tremulous Shade, a Thing Unmade,
Stood Lost by the silent Sea;
And shuddering fought the o'erwhelming thought
Of Its own Identity.

Is the frenzied form that derides the storm
A ghost of the days to Be?
And the restless wave but the troubled grave
Of Its own dread Imagery?
Or merely a wraith cast up without faith
From the jaws of a Phantom Sea?

To his Love Unborn in that grey dim Dawn
Did the Shade of the Dreamer flee;
Nor marked he the Flood where the Vision had stood
Which mocks for Eternity.
For the Soul he would wed was the Hope that had fled
In the battle with Destiny.

Appeared in ***The Equinox Vol. I No. IV*** and in ***The Whirlpool,*** where it was dedicated "*To Bunco*" (Her husband Eugene Wieland).

The Felons' Fortress

Maimed Shadows move athwart the murky air,
Pale prayer-deluded phantoms that the gloom
Delights to cherish – as the hemlock 'd tomb
The corpse of one whose life was scarce more fair
Than that of the grim ghouls who laid him there;
Stripped of all covering till the Day of Doom,
Gaunt as the carrion where the gallows loom,
Unhallowed Imagery of Man's Despair.

As night moths flutter round the taper's head,
As vampires clamour o'er the smitten dead
So madly whirls the wind. The midnight hour
Is fraught with fears more gruesome than yon tower,
Where sin-gorged souls on curdling crimes have fed;
The deep moat shuddering at the armed horde's power.

Appeared in ***The Whilrpool*** and as a typescript, hand dated June 1909.

Death! the Miser.

A miser creeps with in the gloom
And, when the day is old,
He hies him to his hoary tomb
And gloats o'er hidden gold.

And first to view of his treasures rare
Comes the gleaming tress of a maiden's hair,
That he shakes from out the mould.
And then the glint of the autumn leaves,
And gold of the silken Summer sheaves,
And the glist'ning tears that April weaves,
He grasps with his fingers cold.

A dread and dastardly thief is he
Who steals the sunshine from off the sea
To store in his sunless hold.
And young and old fear his icy grip,
As through the forest with smiling lip,
He stalks the shadows that round him slip,
To darken the silent wold.

But most he loves in the haunts of men
Some frail old sinner of four score ten
Who dotes on his wealth untold.
The grim old miser just laughs with glee,
Then pockets his final ghastly fee,
Whilst a doomed soul shrieks from Eternity,
For Life, - that his greed has sold!

Included in her submission to ***The Festival of Britain (Arts Council of Great Britain)***, which has a footnote: "*Written September 9th 1909.*" As a manuscript only.

LOVE POEMS

Circe

Her mouth a rosebud of delight
Low-laughing ‘mid the languid curls,
Whose kissing cadence seems to cite
The rhythmic melody of Night.
Her hair a saraband where whirls
A wanton witch, whose perfumes smite
The shuddering air; a summer night
Where summer lightning darts and curls.

Her soul a Parian marble shrine,
Centered in lily-cups that fold
Their carven petals, smooth and cold,
Far o’er a lake of frozen wine –
Yet deep within whose inmost fold
Sleepeth a snake: the crystal brine
Of endless sorrow seals his shrine;
Wiser than Sin is he, so old!

Appeared in ***The Equinox Vol. I No. VI*** and as a typescript (1910).

An Idyll of Dawn

The dark sea moans to the deaf shore,
The dead sea-wind is out of tune,
And like a hollow lamp, the moon
Lies flickering on the star-strewn floor.

(That late as some fair Maenad glowed,
Swift traversing the Halls of Night.
A meteor spanned her forehead bright,
And comets for her tresses flowed.)

For her the white foam Nereids bore
Pale flowering gems, but all in vain,
Since ever was her bounty fain
To scatter wide those pearls she wore.

Far on the swart Night's Ethiop skin
She scattered them – till Day had drawn
His fiery cohorts of the Dawn,
To compass her and all her Sin.

So – he approaches – in the East
His spear drips blood; the stars grow pale,
There is a murmur in the gale
Which speaks of vengeance dire, increased.

The wan moon sickens – Night has fled
To dimmer regions, fiery pale,
And all ensanguined glows the veil
His late love quickened. He has sped,

Vile cowardly traitor to the last,
To that dark world where shadows dwell,
Safe-fortressed in the heart of Hell,
Where none may look on him aghast.

What matter! Day has triumphed! Soon
His torch shall light the corpse-cold pyre
That dead love presses; swift and dire
Shall be his vengeance, and the noon

Shall find no traces. Swifter, higher,
Leaps the destroying flame; the fire
Curls fierce-caressing, like a brood
Of famished scorpions, sun-imbued

And sunlight-dazzled; bodies nude
As molten metals that have wooed
White shimmering heat: till one vast spire
Shivers the blue – 'tis Dawn's desire!

Appeared in ***The English Review*** (April 1914).

Song

Aphrodite to Sappho

Come, Love, awaken! O'er the wild salt sea,
Shadows strange-shapen whirl themselves and flee
As eddying mist, by storm winds overtaken,
And sunbeams kissed – the shafts all curled and shaken
In shuddering ecstasy!
Come, Love, nor list to tired dreams that twist
Thy lithe long limbs in fierce abandonment,
Awake, and learn of me the secret of the sea,
Whose meaning is the sum of all things blent
In fiercest harmony.

Soft winds are calling on the cloudy deep
(Like foam-flowers falling from the breasts of Sleep
Their Lotus-kiss is). Such a world forestalling
Of wanton blisses, that the fear of palling
Makes e'en the Sirens weep.
Ah me! What serpent hisses from out those purple
　　'bysses,
Far in the womb of the lone-lying sea.
She wakes! Nor dare he creep back to her soul, whence
　　Sleep
Has torn aside the mist-hung drapery;
Too strange the way – and steep.

Appeared in ***The English Review*** (July 1921).

At Seventeen

Laughing I ask you "Why"? And for an answer,
You toss your wild blown tresses to the wind.
Then lightly run as some aerial dance
To where the purple clematis has twined
Its leafy lengths around the pillared porch;
That softly gleams as starlight through the dusk
When each small gnome has lit his yellow torch
And each small elf sleeps in his barley husk.

Lightly you run before, and peering down
Beneath a sheltering canopy of leaves,
You watch my swift advancing with a frown, -
Then like a startled deer when it receives
Its first faint note of warning, glance around,
Wave hands in sweet adieu and turn to fly, -
Alas, too late a refuge you have found.
And greet your ardent captor with a cry.

A prisoner held fast within my arm,
I spell-bound gaze in two deep violet eyes,
Mysterious as lakes in summer calm
Cross which the uncertain shadow softly flies.
I gaze, and from two soft unwilling lips
Artfully steal a kiss, yet one kiss more,
Before from my unwary grasp she slips,
Like to the fabled mermaid on the shore!

O Maiden, with the wildly waving tresses
Draped in your clinging gown of spotless white;
Maiden divine, whose soft and warm caresses

Are given with such sweet and strange affright!
You are to us as music, laughter, singing,
Embodiment of youth's most brightest store,
We watch you – then the distant bells are ringing
And vision fades upon the farther shore.

From two manuscript copies with Ethel Archer's notes on the poem:

"At Seventeen" was written when the author was 14 ½.

Originally the last line was "And one enraptured leads you from the door" which might be used still if preferred. + I had "marriage bells" instead of "distant bells". Please use them if preferred.

PASTORAL POEMS

Storm and Sunrise

As a bird of sable plumage
Rising from a stormy ocean,
Sweeps the Night across the hilltops.
Ruffled are his shining feathers,
All his wings are dashed with water,
Drop which falling dull earth's torches,
Drown the stars in all their glory.
Then the pale-faced moon in terror,
Draws a veil across her features,
Bows her weeping head in silence,
Praying for the stars her children.
But the Night recks naught of sorrow,
Scornfully he rushes onward,
Shakes his crested head in anger,
Fixes flaming eyes upon him;
Yet the Night draws on undaunted.
Mocks the Sun-god in his fortress,
Cries: "O wherefore hid'st thou, Sun-god?
Fearest thou to meet thine equal?"
Then in great and awful anger
Flashing from his cave, the Sun-god
Bursts upon him in his fury.
Shoots him with a golden arrow.
And the Night in sinking downward
Splashes with his blood the Sun-god,
Dyes his yellow locks with crimson,
Stains the snow upon the hilltops.
Then the mortals in the valley
Laugh, and cry: "Behold the Sun-god!
See him flaming on the mountains,

See the Night our foeman burning,
Praise the Sun-god in his triumph!”

Appeared in ***The Whirlpool.***

Sunrise and Sunset

The sun his golden Chariot drives afar,
Chasing with lightning beams the morning star,
And gloom and shadows swiftly flee away
From him, the mighty monarch of the day.

All things on earth attest sweet summer's reign,
The hawthorn opes her fair white bud again,
Within each jewelled cup a dew-drop lies,
Its rainbow luster borrowed from the skies.

The blackbird blithely carols forth his song,
Wafted the scented woodland all along,
And echoed in some joyful lover's heart,
Who with his blushing queen now walks apart.

On the still air breathes not a single word
Save when the cuckoo's mournful note is heard,
And sweet may-blossoms, lately fully blown,
Float softly, airily and lightly down.

Behind the distant hills he goes to rest,
Like some bright bird into a downy nest
Of crimson cloudlets, fringed with richest gold,
And purple-mantled waves with silv'ry fold.

Fair smiling Day has fled in rosy light,
Yielding a way to starry-kirtled Night,
Whose jewelled garment sweeps the vault of Heaven,
While myriad orbs look down, the darkness riven.

So, silence steals o'er the broad ocean deep,
And town and village soon are plunged into sleep,
Waiting Aurora in the flush of dawn,
To paint with fairest hues the coming morn.

Appeared in ***The Whirlpool.***

Elf Song

Song of Shepherds returning through the wood

Light spun gems o'er the green starred moss
Float the fairies and elves across.
Harebell streamers the winds that toss,
Earth in ecstasy scorning. –

Silver streamlet that mocks the blue,
Laughing leaves that the sun looks through,
Say! Where gather the elfin crew
In the heart of the morning?

By the grotto I know so well,
Armed legions methinks do dwell,
Silent shadows, whose sentinel
Gives to mortal scant warning!

For within in the fairy dell
Lies the Lady whose charms we tell,
Witch-elf beauty and woodland spell
More than witchcraft adorning!

Tangled meadows, her waving hair,
Crocus garland her limbs to snare;
Blue bell kisses, her eyelids rare
As eve's hyacinth awning!

O what joy as the far faint rune
Steals anew from the cold bright moon,
Just to dance in a mazy swoon,
Till the grey of the dawning!

Included in her submission to ***The Festival of Britain (Arts Council of Great Britain)*** and as two versions of typescript.

Midsummer Eve

Faint shadows cross the shifting spears of light,
Pale gold and amethyst or warmly white –
Till velvet shod, unseen, the wizard hours
Hold thus their elfin court amid the flowers,
    That wake to winged music of the night.
And silken sighs scarce stir the amorous bowers,
Where passioned Sleep his poppy-garland showers,
    In dreams which mock the hastening moments'
        flight.

Up soars the moon, and higher still and higher
The dancers leap to catch some fairy fire
    To steal and prison in the glow-worm's tail,
    For pixie torches should the starlight fail,
Reflecting gems which deck the elfin choir, -
    Melting like snow-flakes at the daybreak pale.

Appeared in ***The Whirlpool*** where it is dedicated "*To Osmond*" and in the ***Equinox Vol. I No. IV.***

VARIOUS POEMS

The Poet Speaks

Lines written on passing through Hammersmith

Dim fragments woven out of many dawns
Come back to me;
Pale ghosts of many a dream.
From lands across the sea,
From dusk, the silence, in memorial elms,
Blue distances,
The clouds at sunrise, and the gleam,
Of running water.

In the night when the Earth sleeps
Ever so softly,
Dreaming her dream of summer –
And the little elves hide in the long grasses
And a blue mist creeps
Out of the valley, stealthily, curiously,
Seeking he tall hills –
I have known it.

I would return – return from whence I came-
I am haunted,
Haunted by the spell of lonely places,
The whisper of many dawns,
The immensity of silence,
The cold stars, the blackness;
I would return.

I hate the town with its ceaseless clatter and noise,
The clang from the street cars,

The flaring lights, the bustle,
The struggling masses: people who want a seat!
My ears are deafened with the sound of the "latest winner,"
I choke at the acrid smell of the unwashed people.

Commerce!
The hideousness of it all!

-Written September 29th, 1921

Included in her submission to ***The Festival of Britain (Arts Council of Great Britain).***

Autumn Musings

Like a flock of brown birds
Circling, whirling, eddying –
The dead leaves drift in a hurricane.
They are caught up suddenly
And are hurled against the sky.
The sky is intensely blue.
The bare smooth branches of the trees
Are wonderfully silhouetted.
They make strange and beautiful lines

I sit on the top of a passing bus,
(Myself out of the picture,)
I see it all as a curious puppet show
Far away and very unreal: -
The people passing into the park,
Like little marionettes
Grotesque and fantastic.
Like the toy stage to a big toy theatre
Hemming them in.

In a distant street
A taxi cab whistle
Sounds shrilly.
Away on Battersea Bridge,
(and the other bridges that I cannot see)
Little coloured cars are passing
Like the targets in a rifle range.
The river rolls on majestically.
Why does it all seem so far away?

And why am I here?

There is a roaring sound in my ears
Like the far off swell of the sea, -
I am infinitely small,
(or is it infinitely great?)
I will try to think this
While descending the steps of the omnibus
And meanwhile the traffic hurries me on

Am I really outside of the picture
Or is the picture outside of me?
Perhaps, one day when I am dead,
I shall be able to understand it!
Can I have spoken aloud?
A burly arm
In a white-braided blue coat sleeve
Seizes me roughly, -
"You nearly was out of the picture <u>that</u> time, Miss!"

From a manuscript dated October 1923.

The Sphinx

Alone I stood amid strange, sandy spaces,
Where silence seemed to swoon.
The sleepless Guardian of the Desert Places,
Smiled ‘neath the sad young moon
The deathless smile that countless climes and ages
Have sought in vain to fathom from Life’s pages,
Since many an ardent fool and wisest sages
First craved the boon.

Long time I stood and marked the moonbeams quiver,
Lighting the yellow sand.
Watched till the very silence seemed to shiver,
Held by some wizard wand!
And, in that Silence deep as Prayer, came stealing
The thought of that slow smile, its truth revealing!
Surely the Sphinx her ignorance was concealing,
Sublime and Grand!

From an undated typescript.

The Endless Quest

I love the wide open spaces
Where land leans down to the sea,
Where the earth with the sky embraces
And the wind and the waves run free –
Where the gorse is with blossom all golden
And sea-birds make minstrelsy,
And the wind tells a tale that is olden
To the grasses, the waves, and me.

I love the glory of sunrise
And the light of the dawn's first beam,
The passion and peace of moonrise
And the stars that softly gleam;
The splendour of things awaking,
The beauty of things at rest,
But most the glory of making
The joy of the Endless Quest.

I love the glory of sunset
And lands of the glowing west,
The passionate peace of moonset
Where holiest hopes have rest;
The wonder of Love's arriving,
The beauty of Love's behest,
But most the glory of striving
And joy of the Endless Quest.

Appeared in ***The Occult Review*** (March 1932).

RELIGIOUS AND MYSTICAL POEMS

Supra-Liminal

1st Voice

"I know that my Redeemer liveth
And that He
In latter days shall stand upon the earth,
And that though worms
Shall destroy this my body,
Even in the flesh
Shall I see God,
Whom mine eyes shall behold and not another."

2nd Voice

"No man can look upon the face of God
And live.
No man hath seen Himself at any time."

So far I read the Riddle
I expound.

1st Voice

"Still I am I.
Half hoped I to escape,
"The measure of the Mind's futility,"
The thing that reasons, hampers, chains one down,
That speaks of Self, opposing Self to Not-Self.
Says "I",
Yet knows not what it speaks of."

2nd Voice

"Why attempt
To talk of things beyond the bounds of speech?
Why not repose in silence?"

1st Voice — "I had hoped
To wrest from God His secret, -
To expand
Beyond the walls of Time and Space,
To be,
Know, do, and see, and feel, and hear all things
In one great moment.
Yet even as I hoped,
I feared the Lighting Flash that would destroy
The barrier betwixt that All and me,
And fearing, I have failed.
I know but that I seek,
But THAT I seek I know not."

2nd Voice — "To be all things thou must absorb all things,
Absorbing must destroy, -
Then what remains
Of all that is, was, shall be then, but One
Rounding itself to Naught.
Life feeds upon Itself,
The axle of the Wheel
Round which the untiring Universe revolves
Itself is motionless.
Retire into thy Self."

1st Voice — "Black Brilliance only!
Blinded by the Light I can see nothing.
Fearing, I have failed:
I can see nothing."

2nd Voice — Is not No-Thing ALL?

Seest thou not that in the final test
All things are one, and One, we know, is All.
The one great circle

Even Infinity
Cannot be measured by the little mind,
Cannot be known by aught but its vast Self.
The finite, could it grasp the infinite,
Losing its sense of small identity,
(Its little separate self)
Would but become the thing it gazed upon;
And in one flash
Annihilating Time and Space, and all
The things that here we know as infinite, -
Even Infinity would cease to be,
The finite would become Infinity,
Infinity the Finite.

Passivity in action,
Action passive:
The perfect Balance,
That knoweth things as they are each to each,
Itself knows not, but is.
(And so we say
"It knows not its own Self
But knows the thing it is not.")
And imperfection may reach unto a possible perfection,
But could perfection know aught but its own self,
Straightway perfection ceases.
So we picture
The serpent swallowing its tail
Fit emblem of Truth beyond all speech;
The endless circle.
Know that thou art, - I am –
And straightway neither is.

The Dawn is breaking, Night has fled away
And Death is Life. The moment of the change
Ever escapes us, and in Time or Space
We cannot place it.
Wherefore we say that in Eternity we solve the
  riddle,
Wherefore to us the immeasurably small and
  great
Are equal concepts,
All is infinite.
Seek not to <u>know</u>, but BE.

From a typescript with hand corrected title, originally titled *Subliminal* and dated 1921. There is also a partial typescript with *?* as the title.

A Patre Unigenitus

From Heaven the Sole-Begotten One
Unspotted through a Virgin came,
Life of the Godhead, God's own Son,
Light of the Unbegotten Flame.
For us He took the form of man,
So human blendeth with divine –
His love creation doth outspan
As light doth o'er the darkness shine.

> The Royal Babe of Bethlehem
> Is born to us this blessed night,
> Hymned by the choir of Seraphim,
> And angels echoing to the height.
> The Royal Babe of Bethlehem
> Sheltered by wings of angels bright,
> Is found of those who worship Him,
> Shepherds and Kings, this hallowed night.

This we, O Saviour, ask of Thee,
Look down of Thy sweet charity,
Remove the darkness of our night
With blessings of Thy healing light.
Thou hast already come, we know
We trust that Thou wilt come again;
Thy famous Kingdom, Lord, do Thou
Guard with Thy shield amain.

> The Royal Babe of Bethlehem
> Is born to us this blessed night,
> Hymned by the choir of Seraphim,

And angels echoing to the height.
The Royal Babe of Bethlehem
Guarded by hosts of angels bright,
Is found of those who welcome Him,
Shepherds and Kings, this wished-for night.

All glory be to Thee, O Lord,
Who hast appeared this day:
Father and Spirit be adored
For endless ages, aye.

From an undated typescript. Ethel Archer's translation (or impression) from the Latin of *A Patre Unigenitus*, a hymn often associated with the Feast of the Epiphany by an unknown author between the 10th and 13th centuries.

Versicle Q. of St Columba's Altus Prosator

Who has ascended Sinai to speak with God the Lord?
Who has heard the [clanging] as of battle trumpets abroad?
Who has heard the thunder beyond the limits of sound?
Who has seen the lightnings in circling flashes [o'er bound]
The mighty rocks in collision? Who has seen them and who the star
That burns in the utmost Heaven, the flame white regions afar?
The Holy and awful Vision the Lord of the Realms of the Light
Who has known Him (ere Day he arisen to vanquish the Hosts of the Night)
Meet with man, face to face as a friend might,
Talk as friend talks with friend on the height?
Who, but Moses, the judge of his people
Moses, the Israelite!

From a manuscript of what Ethel Archer called a "*free translation*" of stanza Q from St. Columba's ***Altus Prosator*** (Irish, 6th Century), which had a stanza for every letter of the alphabet.

Vesper Hymn

Now gently, softly falls the Light
And earthly things withdraw from sight
And round us falls the hush of night:
        Its calm and peace.

With lowly reverence let us pray
For pardon where we've gone astray
And left the Father's holy way
        That leads to peace.

His children all to Him are dear,
He dwells not far away, but near –
O hush, my soul, the Lord is <u>here</u>!
        He whispers "Peace!"

From an undated typescript.

At the Tenth Hour
The Dying Robber Soliloquises

"I have trodden the lonely places,
I have entered where none durst follow:
I have walked the highways with Death;
Death has feasted with me.

Death is to me no stranger!
We have communed of old together;
Why should I fear him now,
Now when there's naught but he?

What said the voice of old?
Life is Death, Death is Life –
It may be, --
Always we see it awry, always we use it amiss.
Life may be Death, viewed crosswise,
O Master
Shall I find Life beyond, Life and a vision free?

See! I make peace with all,
With God, and the world, my brothers;
Nothing remains to me, of earth or of earthly care;
Light is enfolding me; Light, and some strange sweet sorrow,
Light is enfolding me! Life! Ah, Lord Christ, I see!"

July 22nd, 1933.

From a typescript.

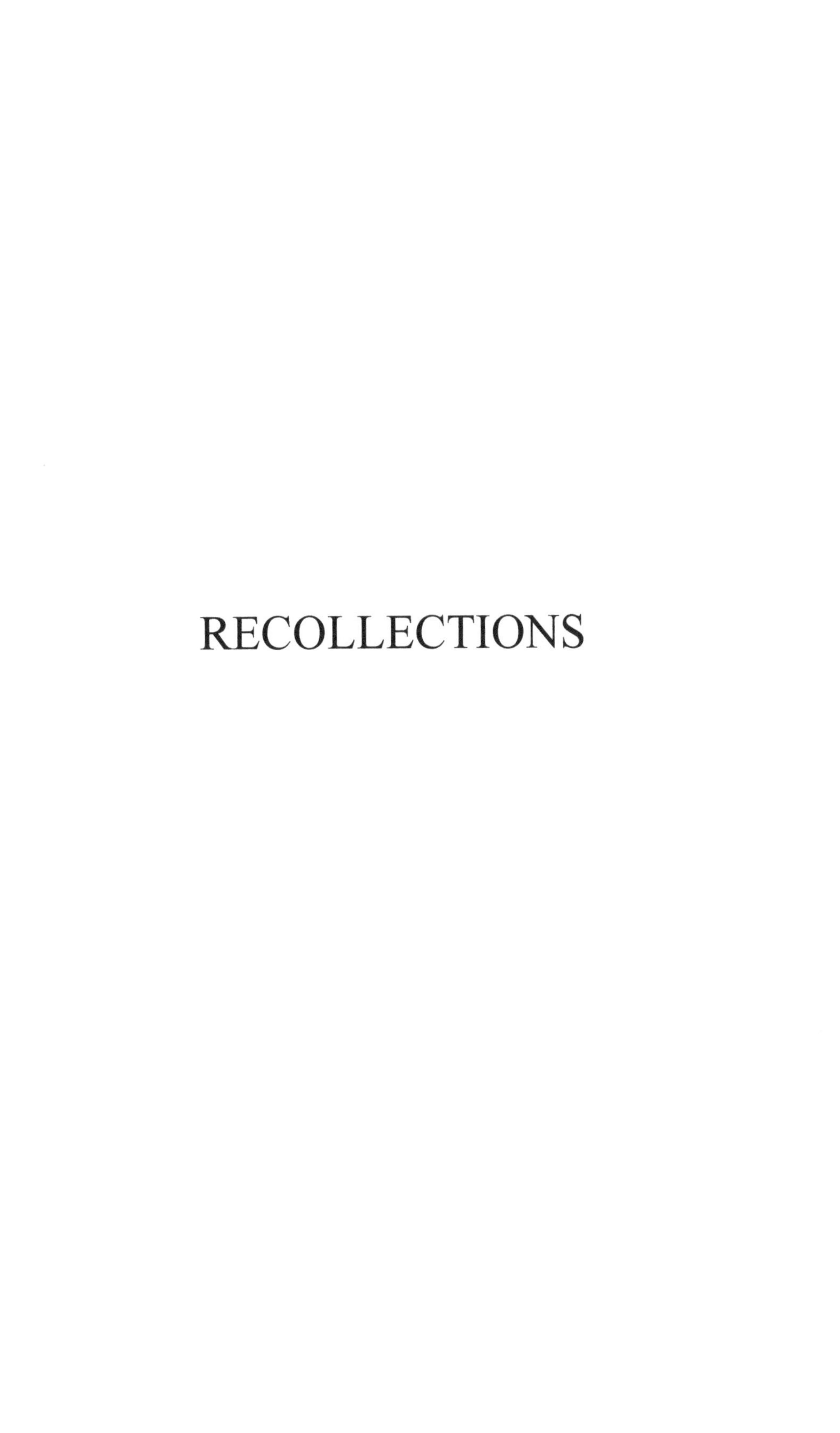

RECOLLECTIONS

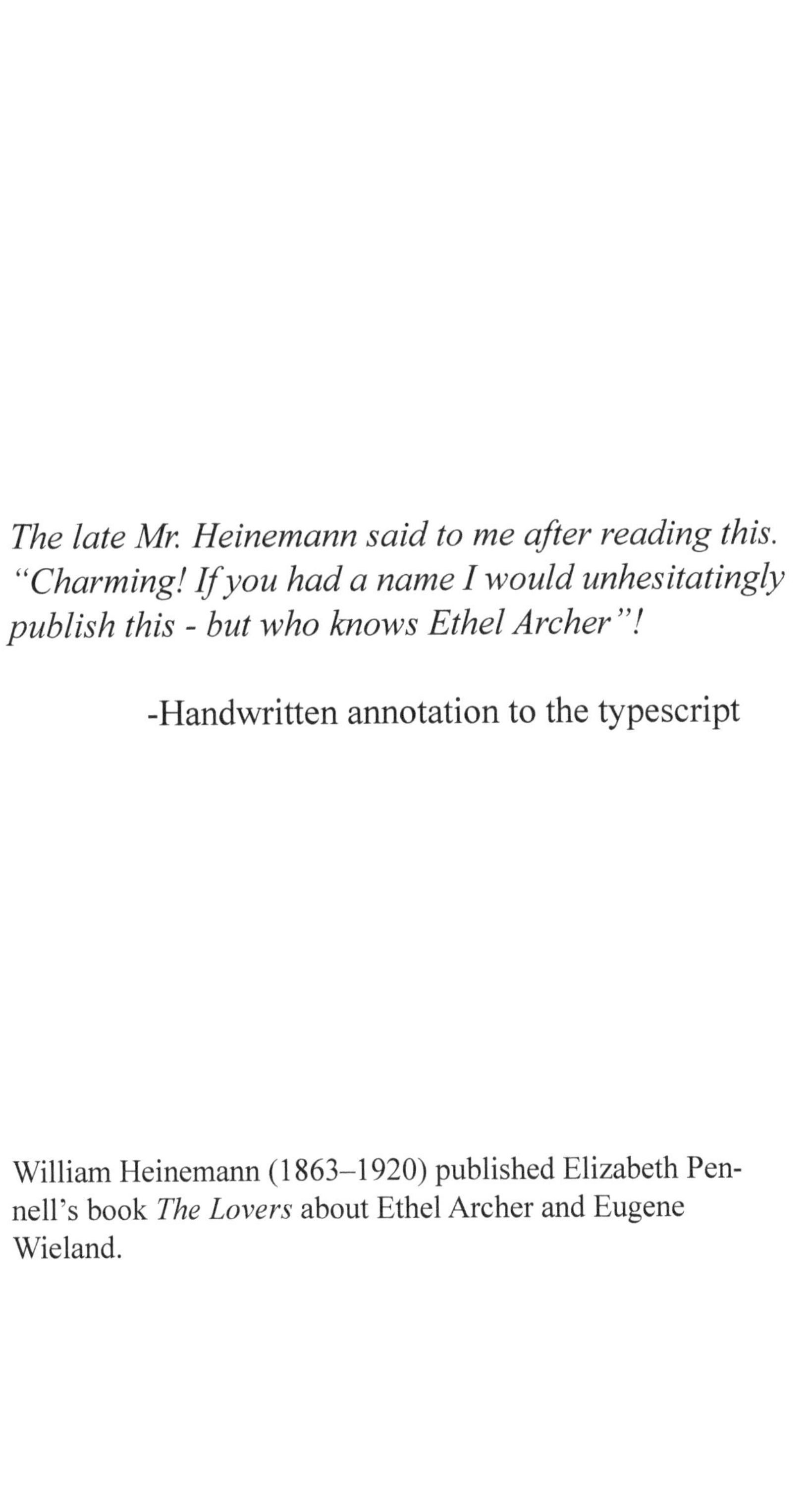

The late Mr. Heinemann said to me after reading this. "Charming! If you had a name I would unhesitatingly publish this - but who knows Ethel Archer"!

-Handwritten annotation to the typescript

William Heinemann (1863–1920) published Elizabeth Pennell's book *The Lovers* about Ethel Archer and Eugene Wieland.

The "Tudor cottage" where Ethel Archer was born. On the verso of the photo she has written: "*The gates have been mended by some subsequent occupier of the cottage.*"

RECOLLECTIONS

by Ethel Archer

The thing that I can most definitely remember from the time I first commenced consciously to record my impressions, was a love of the Beautiful. A love so intense that it almost verged on an ache.

And mixed with this love was the sense of sorrow: that vague intangible unhappiness amounting at times almost to a prevision of calamity, that is never far distant from the most beautiful summer days, and that broods like an image of pain over the peaceful hills and slumbering valleys, and is all the more strongly felt in that it is never defined.

One realized vaguely that one was seeing it all for the last time, and insignificant details impressed one with a curious intensity whilst in the innermost depths of one's being a voice said: "Such and such a thing you will remember years afterwards."

How true I have since found this!

The scent of clover, the song of the lark above the cornfields, the shadow of the clouds (idly chasing each other as they darken momentarily the face of the wind-swept downs), a certain gravel path and the hot scent of geraniums, the vivid scarlet blooms striking as violent a note of colour as the blare of a trumpet, and uttering a brazen challenge to the vault of the blue, remorseless sky!

Are not these the memories inextricably interwoven with school days and the age of twelve?

And then -

Buttercups, cow-parsley, the faraway voices of children playing in a neighbouring field; the chirping of grasshoppers, and a sense of myriad insect life; butterflies, and the cawing of rooks overhead, and with it all a sense of beautiful remoteness - and am I not an infant again?

I fancy that all our earliest recollections must be linked with flowers. I know that my own are, and it is interesting to note, how, with the advance of years, our favourite flower (if we chance to have one) invariably alters, and how seldom, if ever, it is primarily the rose!

I think that my earliest love was the Tiger-Lily (surely the Circus-Queen among flowers) and I doubt not that she filled me with as much awe and admiration as the Lady of the Ring herself; whose agile grace and fine disregard of danger, as she leapt through the flaming hoop nimbly to alight on the back of the fattest and prettiest of white horses, I had already secretly determined to emulate.

I remember King, the gardener, for whom at this time I had conceived a great attachment, giving me one fine morning one of the tawny trumpet-shaped flowers and for three whole days I guarded it jealously in a glass. (It would perhaps be as well to remark at this juncture that I had reached the mature age of four & a half years!)

I never dared to pick one, why I cannot say - for there were many in the garden; and I was not in the least afraid of the Canterbury Bells, Irises, Moon-daisies, or in fact any of the other flowers! But it always seemed to me that the Tiger-Lily was very conscious, and that she had the same terrible "awareness" that I have since learned to associate with and dread in the eye of the larger snakes.

From snakes to worms is not so big a stretch of the imagination.

I can still remember the thrill of horror that ran through me, when King, the gardener having accidentally chopped asunder a long fat worm (one of the kind with pink swollen ridges) explained casually in answer to my sympathetic shiver: "Lord! Missie, that doesn't hurt them! Why, if you was to cut him in two, each worm would grow into another worm, and if you cut the halves again, each half again would be a worm!"

Instantly I did a rapid mental calculation which filled the universe with worms!

With a shudder I was forcibly wrenched away from my thoughts the possibility of ever beholding so unpleasant a spectacle, and busied myself with other matters. King, who when he chanced to be in a noncommunicative mood, had strange lapses of silence, chewed with thoughtful thoroughness a sprig of mint (much as an ostler chews a straw) and I especially remember that this was the case when he happened to be planting potatoes!

The obvious connection between the two was, I am convinced, unconscious: but for me, I fancied that chewing mint must be a necessary part of the performance of gardening, - and I, too, wandered about sucking away at a green leaf with much solemnity, until checked by my grandmother, who suddenly appearing one morning to watch operations, demanded to know what that nasty looking weed was the child was sucking, and that it be taken away from her.

Note:-

I had intended writing a series of articles shewing the favourite colours, flowers, pastimes & so on which I associated with different ages. - The flowers started tiger-lily, passion-flower, water-lily & so on The colours, green & silver, for a very long time, & now almost exclusively pale gold.

E.f.W

Genuine Tudor Cottage
Where Ethel Archer was born.

The gables have been [illegible] by some subsequent occupier of the cottage

www.ingramcontent.com/pod-product-compliance
Ingram Content Group UK Ltd.
Pitfield, Milton Keynes, MK11 3LW, UK
UKHW041643190726
13854UKWH00006B/2678